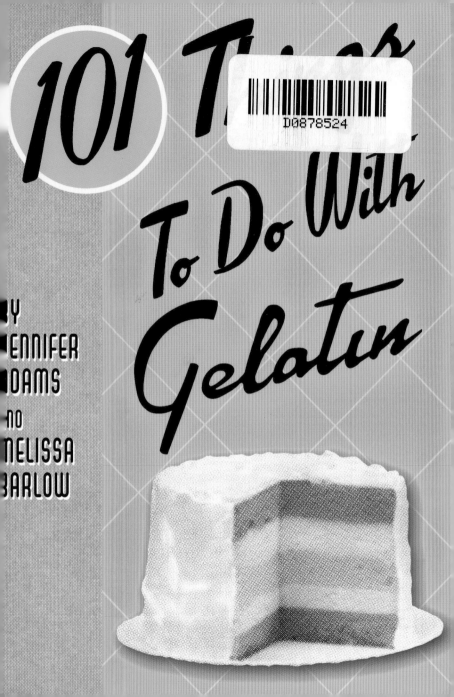

101 Things To Do With Gelatin

BY
JENNIFER
ADAMS
AND
MELISSA
BARLOW

101 Things To Do With Gelatin

101 Things To Do With Gelatin

BY
JENNIFER ADAMS AND
MELISSA BARLOW

GIBBS SMITH
TO ENRICH AND INSPIRE HUMANKIND
Salt Lake City | Charleston | Santa Fe | Santa Barbara

First Edition
12 11 10 09 08   5 4 3 2 1

Published by
Gibbs Smith
P.O. Box 667
Layton, Utah 84041

1.800.835.4993 orders
www.gibbs-smith.com

Printed and bound in Korea

Library of Congress Cataloging-in-Publication Data

Adams, Jennifer.
  101 things to do with gelatin / Jennifer Adams and Melissa Barlow. — 1st ed.
    p. cm.
  ISBN-13: 978-1-4236-0247-7
  ISBN-10: 1-4236-0247-1
  1. Cookery (Gelatin) I. Barlow, Melissa. II. Title. III. Title: One hundred one things to do with gelatin. IV. Title: One hundred and one things to do with gelatin.
  TX814.5.G4A33 2008
  641.8'64—dc22
                    2008004277

For Nancene Facer, my Aunt Nanny, who taught me how to make a great Jell-O salad—and infinitely more. —J.A.

For Todd and everyone in both of our families for being good sports and taste-testing my recipes at every dinner, party, or other family gathering for so many months! —M.B.

CONTENTS

Pies

Fluffy Strawberry Pie 64 • Orange-Lemon Pie 65 • Strawberry Yogurt Pie 66 • Frozen Lemonade Pie 67 • Key Lime Pie 68 • Pineapple Cream Cheese Pie 69 • Cherry-Lemon Cream Cheese Pie 70 • Mandarin Orange Pie 71 • Pretty Spring Pie 72 • Favorite Peach Pie 73 • Raspberry Danish Pie 74 • Frozen Cherry Pie 75 • Creamy Cranberry Pie 76 • Frozen Black-Bottom Raspberry Pie 77

Spoon Desserts

Easy Cheesecake 80 • Strawberry Cheesecake Squares 81 • Key Lime Dessert 82 • Raspberry Cream Dessert 83 • Lemon Sherbet Squares 84 • Lemon Soufflé 85 • Strawberry Trifle 86 • Cherry Cobbler 87 • Peach Crisp 88 • Creamy Pudding 89 • Peachy Frozen Yogurt 90 • Raspberry Ice Cream 91 • Strawberry-Banana Ice Cream 92 • Lime Sorbet 93 • Red Hot Dessert 94 • Caramel Apple Squares 95 • Rainbow Dessert 96 • Strawberry Pretzel Dessert 97

Just for Fun

Edible Fish Bowl 100 • Apple Chips 101 • Crispy Rice Squares 102 • Gummy Lollipops 103 • Fruity Popsicles 104 • Double-Orange Pops 105 • Popcorn Balls 106 • Apricot Sugar Cookies 107 • Lemon Poppy Seed Cookies 108 • Cookie Swirls 109 • Strawberry Pizza 110 • Mormon Salad 111 • Finger Jell-O 112

Drinks

Banana Whip 114 • Purple Cow 115 • Orange Julius 116 • Cherry Lemonade Slush 117 • Sweet-and-Sour Berry Slush 118 • Orange-Pineapple Colada 119 • Cran-Raspberry Punch 120 • Icy Lemon-Lime Refresher 121 • Raspberry Smoothie 122 • Bumble Shakes 123

FUN FACTS

- More than a million packages of Jell-O brand gelatin are purchased every day.

- Fruits that sink in gelatin include grapes and fruits in heavy syrup, such as fruit cocktail, peaches, and pears.

- Fruits that float in gelatin include fresh fruit such as bananas, oranges, and apples.

- Sugar-free Jell-O was first available in 1984.

- Jell-O was inducted into the Smithsonian Institute in 1991.

- In 1996, astronaut Shannon Lucid took gelatin dessert to the Mir space station.

- As immigrants passed through Ellis Island, they were often served a bowl of gelatin as a treat to welcome them to America.

- When hooked up to an electroencephalograph machine—an instrument that records the electrical activity of the brain—gelatin demonstrates movement virtually identical to the brain waves of a healthy adult.

- Gelatin served as a blood plasma substitute during World War II.

- Jack Benny and Bill Cosby were both spokesmen for Jell-O products.

- A cut-up Jell-O box was used as evidence in the trial of spies Julius and Ethel Rosenberg.

- Peter Cooper obtained the first American patent for gelatin in 1845.

- In 1895, cough syrup manufacturer Pearl B. Wait purchased the patent for gelatin and developed a packaged gelatin dessert.

- Wait's wife, May David Wait, named the dessert "Jell-O."

- Gelatin is used to make the outer shells for capsules in the pharmaceutical industry.

- A new application for gelatin is in the paint ball industry, which uses it to construct paint balls.

- Most of the gelatin produced is eaten in gelatin desserts, marshmallows, and gummy candies.

- The residents of Salt Lake City eat more lime-flavored gelatin than residents of any other city in the U.S.

- The original gelatin dessert flavors were orange, lemon, strawberry, and raspberry.

- Gelatin dessert flavors that flopped include celery, coffee, cola, and chocolate.

FRUIT SALADS

POMEGRANATE SALAD

I large box	**cherry or black cherry gelatin**
2 cups	**boiling water**
2 cups	**cold pomegranate juice**
I container (8 ounces)	**frozen whipped topping,** thawed
$1/2$ cup	**sliced almonds or chopped walnuts**
$1/2$ to I cup	**fresh pomegranate seeds***

Dissolve gelatin in boiling water. Add pomegranate juice. Pour into a 9 x 13-inch baking pan and chill until set. Spread whipped topping over top and then sprinkle with nuts and pomegranate seeds. Makes 10–12 servings.

*If pomegranate is not in season, just eliminate.

ORANGE-BERRY SALAD

1 large box	**raspberry or strawberry gelatin**
2 cups	**boiling water**
1 package (12 ounces)	**frozen raspberries**
2	**bananas,** sliced
3/4 cup	**chopped pecans or walnuts**
1	**orange,** juiced

In a large bowl, dissolve gelatin in boiling water. Add frozen berries and stir until thawed. Add bananas, nuts, and orange juice. Mix well and chill until set. Makes 10–12 servings.

PEACHES AND CREAM

I large box	**peach gelatin**
2 cups	**boiling water**
2 cups	**cold water**
3 to 4	**fresh peaches,** pitted, peeled, and diced*
I container (8 ounces)	**frozen whipped topping,** thawed

Dissolve gelatin in boiling water. Add cold water and then pour into a 9 x 13-inch pan. Chill until partially set, about 45 minutes to I hour, and then stir in fruit. Chill until set. Spread whipped topping over top. Makes 10–12 servings.

*2 to 3 cans (15 ounces each) peaches, drained and diced, may be substituted.

SPARKLING BERRY SALAD

1 large box	**blackberry fusion gelatin***
1 1/2 cups	**boiling water**
1 1/2 cups	**lemon-lime soda**
3 cups	**fresh mixed berries or frozen mixed berries,** thawed
1 container (8 ounces)	**frozen whipped topping,** thawed

In an 8 x 8-inch pan, dissolve gelatin in boiling water. Stir in soda. Chill until partially set, about 45 minutes to 1 hour. Add fruit and then chill until set. Spread whipped topping over top. Makes 9 servings.

*Any berry flavor gelatin may be substituted.

MELON WITH STRAWBERRIES

1 large box **watermelon gelatin**
2 cups **boiling water**
2 cups **cold water**
1 container (8 ounces) **frozen whipped topping,** thawed
2 cups **sliced fresh strawberries**

Dissolve gelatin in boiling water. Add cold water. Pour into a 9 x 13-inch pan and chill until firm. Top gelatin with fresh strawberries and then spread whipped topping over top. Makes 10–12 servings.

STRAWBERRY-KIWI SALAD

1 large box	**strawberry-kiwi gelatin**
2 cups	**boiling water**
1 1/2 cups	**ice**
1	**banana,** thinly sliced
12 to 14	**strawberries,** sliced
1 container (8 ounces)	**frozen whipped topping,** thawed
4	**kiwifruit,** peeled and thinly sliced

Dissolve gelatin in boiling water. Stir in ice and then refrigerate until partially set, about 45 minutes. Stir in banana. Pour into an 8 x 8-inch pan and then chill until firm. Place a layer of strawberries over set gelatin. Spread whipped topping over strawberries and then garnish with kiwifruit slices over top. Makes 9 servings.

DR. PEPPER SALAD

I can (16 ounces)	**sweet black cherries**
I tablespoon	**fresh lemon juice**
2 small boxes	**black cherry gelatin**
I can (12 ounces)	**cold Dr. Pepper**
I can (8 ounces)	**crushed pineapple**
1/2 pint	**whipping cream,** whipped and sweetened

Drain liquid from cherries and reserve. Slice cherries in half and set aside. Combine reserved liquid with lemon juice and enough water to make 2 cups. Place in a medium saucepan and bring to a boil. Completely dissolve gelatin in boiling liquid and then stir in Dr. Pepper. Pour into a 9 x 13-inch pan and refrigerate until gelatin turns syrupy, about 45 minutes. Fold cherries and pineapple with juice into the gelatin. Chill until firm. Top with whipped cream. Makes 12 servings.

COCA-COLA SALAD

1 can (16 ounces)	**Bing cherries**
1 large box	**cherry gelatin**
1 can (12 ounces)	**cold Coca-Cola**
1 can (20 ounces)	**crushed pineapple**
1 cup	**chopped walnuts**

Drain liquid from cherries and reserve. Slice cherries in half and set aside. Add enough water to cherry juice to make 2 cups. Bring to a boil. In a 9 x 13-inch pan, pour boiling liquid over gelatin. Stir to dissolve, at least 2 minutes. Stir in Coca-Cola. Refrigerate until partially set, about 45 minutes. Fold in cherries, pineapple with juice, and walnuts. Chill until set. Makes 12 servings.

CRAN-APPLE SALAD

1 small box **strawberry gelatin**
1 can (16 ounces) **whole berry cranberry sauce**
1 1/2 cups **chunky applesauce**

Dissolve gelatin in boiling water. Stir in cranberry sauce until smoothly blended. Stir in applesauce. Pour into an 8 x 8-inch pan and chill until firm. Makes 9 servings.

CRAN-RASPBERRY LAYERS

1 large box	**raspberry gelatin**
1¾ cups	**boiling water**
1 can (20 ounces)	**crushed pineapple**
1 can (16 ounces)	**whole-berry cranberry sauce**
1 cup	**sour cream**

In a bowl, dissolve gelatin in boiling water. Add pineapple with juice and cranberry sauce, stirring until cranberry sauce is well blended. Chill until partially set, about 45 minutes. Pour half of the gelatin mixture into an 8 x 8-inch pan. Chill until firm. Let the remaining gelatin stand at room temperature. Stir in the sour cream and then spread evenly over the firm gelatin. Chill until firm. Cut into squares. Makes 9 servings.

RASPBERRY PARFAIT

1 large box **raspberry gelatin**
1/2 pint **whipping cream,** whipped and sweetened
1 pint **fresh raspberries**

In a trifle bowl, make gelatin according to package directions. When gelatin is set, top with whipped cream and decorate with fresh berries. Makes 12–15 servings.

TROPICAL JEWEL SALAD

1 can (11 ounces) **mandarin oranges**
1 can (8 ounces) **pineapple tidbits**
1 small box **orange gelatin**
1 cup **cold water**
$^1/_4$ cup **flaked coconut** (optional)

Drain mandarin oranges and pineapple; reserve juice. Combine juices and water to make 1 cup, if needed, and bring to a boil. Pour boiling mixture into gelatin and stir until completely dissolved, at least 2 minutes. Add cold water. Pour into an 8 x 8-inch pan and chill until partially set, about 30–40 minutes. Gently fold in fruit and coconut if using. Return to refrigerator until completely set. Makes 9 servings.

SIMPLE RASPBERRY SQUARES

1 large box	**raspberry gelatin**
2 cups	**boiling water**
1 package (12 ounces)	**frozen raspberries**
2 cups	**cold water**
1/2 pint	**whipping cream,** whipped and sweetened
1/2 cup	**chopped walnuts**

Dissolve gelatin in boiling water, stirring at least 2 minutes. Add frozen berries and stir until thawed. Add cold water and pour into a 9 x 13-inch pan. Chill until set. Top with whipped cream and sprinkle with chopped walnuts. Cut into squares and serve. Makes 12 servings.

BERRY ORANGE KISSES

1 small box **raspberry gelatin**
1 can (11 ounces) **mandarin oranges,** drained
2 cups **fresh raspberries**

Make gelatin according to package directions. Chill in a medium-size bowl, about 30 to 45 minutes. When partially set, gently fold in oranges and raspberries. Chill until firm. Makes 9 servings.

APRICOT PARFAIT

2 cans (15 ounces each) **diced apricots**
2 small boxes **apricot gelatin**
$^1/_2$ teaspoon **lemon extract**
2 cups **cold water**
$^1/_2$ pint **whipping cream,** whipped and sweetened
$^1/_2$ cup **chopped walnuts**

Drain apricots and reserve juice. Add enough water to make 2 cups and bring to a boil. Dissolve gelatin in hot liquid, stirring constantly for at least 2 minutes. Stir in lemon extract and then cold water. Pour into a large glass bowl or trifle bowl, and chill until set. When gelatin is completely set, gently top with drained apricots. Carefully top with whipped cream and then garnish with walnuts. Makes 12 servings.

SWEET CHERRY PIE SALAD

I large box	**cherry gelatin**
2 cups	**boiling water**
I can (20 ounces)	**crushed pineapple**
I can (20 ounces)	**cherry pie filling**
I package (8 ounces)	**cream cheese,** softened
I container (8 ounces)	**sour cream**
$^1/_2$ cup	**sugar**
I teaspoon	**vanilla**

Dissolve gelatin in boiling water. Add pineapple with juice and pie filling and mix well. Chill until set in a 9 x 13-inch pan.

In a bowl, blend cream cheese, sour cream, sugar, and vanilla until smooth. Spread over set gelatin and serve. Makes 12 servings.

CREAMY FRUIT SALADS

BLUEBERRY CREAM CHEESE SALAD

2 small boxes **raspberry gelatin**
2 cups **boiling water**
1 can (16 ounces) **blueberries**
1 can (8 ounces) **crushed pineapple**
1 package (8 ounces) **cream cheese,** softened
1 pint **whipping cream,** whipped and sweetened

Dissolve gelatin in boiling water. Stir in blueberries and pineapple with their juice. Mash in cream cheese with a fork or potato masher until mostly blended. Chill in a 9 x 13-inch pan until partially set, about 40 minutes. Fold half the whipped cream into the salad and chill until completely set. Top with remaining whipped cream before serving. Makes 12 servings.

CREAMY STRAWBERRY SALAD

1 large box	**strawberry gelatin**
3 1/2 cups	**boiling water**
2 packages (16 ounces each)	**frozen strawberries,** thawed
1 pint	**whipping cream,** whipped and sweetened

Dissolve gelatin in boiling water. Stir in strawberries. Chill in a 9 x 13-inch pan until partially set, about 40 minutes. Fold in half the whipped cream. Chill until completely set. Top with remaining whipped cream and serve. Makes 12 servings.

DOUBLE-LAYER CITRUS SALAD

I large box	**orange gelatin**
I small box	**Cook & Serve lemon pudding**
3 cans (15 ounces each)	**mandarin oranges,** drained
I small box	**lemon instant pudding**
I container (8 ounces)	**frozen whipped topping,** thawed

Make orange gelatin according to package directions and then set aside, but do not put in refrigerator to set. Make the Cook & Serve lemon pudding according to package directions. Combine liquid orange gelatin and cooked lemon pudding with a wire whisk or hand mixer until smooth.

Layer the mandarin oranges in the bottom of a 9 x 13-inch glass dish (extra deep if available). Next pour the gelatin-pudding mixture over top and smooth with a spoon. Refrigerate overnight until set.

Make the lemon instant pudding according to package directions. Fold the whipped topping into the pudding and then spread over the set gelatin-pudding mixture. Refrigerate 1–2 more hours before serving. Makes 12–14 servings.

LEMONADE SALAD

1 large box	**lemon gelatin**
2 cups	**boiling water**
1 cup	**sugar**
1/2 teaspoon	**salt**
1 can (12 ounces)	**frozen lemonade concentrate,** slightly thawed
1 container (12 ounces)	**frozen whipped topping,** thawed
4 to 6	**kiwifruit,** peeled and thinly sliced

In a large bowl, dissolve gelatin in boiling water. Add sugar and salt. Add lemonade and stir until melted. Refrigerate until syrupy, about 45 minutes to 1 hour. Fold in a little more than half of the whipped topping and pour into a 9 x 13-inch pan. Refrigerate until set and then spread remaining whipped topping over top. Arrange sliced kiwifruit over whipped topping. Makes 10–12 servings.

RASPBERRY LEMONADE SQUARES

I package (12 ounces)	**frozen raspberries,** thawed
I large box	**raspberry gelatin**
2 cups	**boiling water**
I pint	**vanilla ice cream**
I small can (6 ounces)	**frozen pink lemonade concentrate,** thawed
I container (8 ounces)	**frozen whipped topping,** thawed

Drain raspberries, reserving syrup. Dissolve gelatin in boiling water. Stir in ice cream by the spoonful until it is melted. Stir in lemonade concentrate and reserved syrup. Refrigerate in a 9 x 13-inch pan until partially set, about 45 minutes. Fold in raspberries. Refrigerate until firmly set and then spread whipped topping over top. Cut into squares before serving. Makes 10–12 servings.

PINEAPPLE-LIME SALAD

1 small box **lime gelatin**
1 container (16 ounces) **cottage cheese**
1 can (8 ounces) **crushed pineapple**
1 container (8 ounces) **frozen whipped topping,** thawed
1/2 cup **chopped walnuts**

Stir dry gelatin mix into cottage cheese. Stir in pineapple with juice. Fold in whipped topping and nuts. Transfer to a serving bowl and chill for at least 4 hours before serving. Makes 8–10 servings.

FROZEN RASPBERRY YOGURT SALAD

I small box **raspberry gelatin**
I cup **boiling water**
I container (6 ounces) **raspberry yogurt**
I cup **fresh or frozen raspberries**
I cup **frozen whipped topping,** thawed

Dissolve gelatin in boiling water. Chill until partially set, about 45 minutes. Fold in yogurt, raspberries, and whipped topping; pour into an 8 x 8-inch pan and freeze until set. Thaw slightly before serving. Makes 6–8 servings.

CINDY'S CREAMY SALAD

I large box	**Cook & Serve vanilla pudding**
I large box	**gelatin,** any flavor
3 cups	**water**
I container (8 ounces)	**frozen whipped topping,** thawed
2 cups	**fresh or frozen raspberries, or mandarin oranges,** drained

Cook pudding, gelatin, and water together in a saucepan until it comes to a boil. Stir well and then let mixture cool. Gently fold in whipped topping and fruit of choice. Pour into a large glass bowl; chill 2–3 hours, or until completely set. Makes 10–12 servings.

YUMMY PEAR SALAD

I can (29 ounces)	**pears,** juice reserved
I small box	**lime gelatin**
I package (8 ounces)	**cream cheese**
I container (8 ounces)	**frozen whipped topping,** thawed

Add enough water to pear juice to equal I cup and bring to a boil. Dissolve gelatin in juice. Place in refrigerator until gelatin just begins to set, about 30 to 40 minutes. In a blender or with a fork, mash pears and cream cheese together until smooth. Gently blend into gelatin. Fold half of the whipped topping into gelatin mixture. Pour into a 2-quart glass dish and chill until set. Top with remaining whipped topping. Makes 7–9 servings.

STRAWBERRY-BANANA SOUR CREAM SALAD

2 small boxes	**strawberry-banana gelatin**
2 cups	**boiling water**
1 package (16 ounces)	**frozen strawberries,** partially thawed
4	**bananas,** thinly sliced
2 cups	**sour cream**

Dissolve gelatin in boiling water. Put half of gelatin mixture in a bowl and put in fridge to partially set, about 35–45 minutes. Add strawberries to remaining gelatin and stir until completely thawed. Stir in bananas. Pour gelatin with fruit into a 9 x 13-inch pan and chill until almost firm.

When gelatin in bowl is partially set, stir in sour cream. Spread mixture over set gelatin in the pan. Refrigerate until set. Makes 12 servings.

ISLAND PINEAPPLE SQUARES

I large box	**island pineapple gelatin**
3 cups	**boiling water**
I can (8 ounces)	**crushed pineapple**
I cup	**cold water**
I package (8 ounces)	**cream cheese,** softened
2 cups	**miniature marshmallows**
I pint	**whipping cream,** whipped and sweetened

In a 9 x 13-inch pan, dissolve gelatin in boiling water. Stir in pineapple with juice and cold water. Mash in cream cheese with fork or potato masher until mostly blended. Stir in marshmallows. Chill until partially set, about 45 minutes. Fold half the whipped cream into the partially set salad and chill until completely set. Top with remaining whipped cream before serving. Makes 12–14 servings.

FROZEN CHAMPAGNE SALAD

I can (20 ounces) **crushed pineapple**
I small box **strawberry-kiwi or strawberry-banana gelatin**
I package (10 ounces) **frozen strawberries**
$1/4$ cup **sugar**
$1/2$ cup **chopped pecans or walnuts** (optional)
I cup **miniature marshmallows**
I container (12 ounces) **frozen whipped topping,** thawed

Mix together pineapple with juice, dry gelatin mix, frozen strawberries, sugar, nuts if using, marshmallows, and whipped topping. Spread in a 9 x 13-inch pan and freeze. Before serving, thaw slightly and cut into squares. Makes 12 servings.

NANNY'S ORANGE FLUFF

1 small box **orange gelatin**
1 container (16 ounces) **cottage cheese**
1 can (11 ounces) **mandarin oranges,** drained
1 can (8 ounces) **crushed pineapple**
1 container (8 ounces) **frozen whipped topping,** thawed

Stir dry gelatin mix into cottage cheese. Partially smash oranges with a fork and then stir into cottage cheese mixture. Add pineapple with juice. Fold in whipped topping. Transfer to a serving bowl and chill for at least 4 hours before serving. Makes 8–10 servings.

VARIATION: Stir in 1 to 2 cups miniature marshmallows and $1/2$ cup chopped nuts.

LEMON PUDDING FRUIT SALAD

1 small box **lemon gelatin**
1 1/2 cups **boiling water**
1 small box **instant lemon or vanilla pudding**
1 cup **frozen whipped topping,** thawed
1 can **fruit cocktail,** drained
2 cans (11 ounces each) **mandarin oranges,** drained
1 can (13 ounces) **pineapple tidbits,** drained
3 **bananas,** sliced

Dissolve gelatin in boiling water and then refrigerate until partially set, about 1 hour. Make pudding according to package directions. Combine pudding, gelatin, and whipped topping. Fold in fruit. Transfer to a serving bowl and refrigerate until set. Makes 14–16 servings.

AMBROSIA SALAD

2 cups	**apricot nectar**
2 small boxes	**orange, peach, or apricot gelatin**
2 cups	**cold water**
2 cans (8 ounces each)	**crushed pineapple**
2 cups	**frozen whipped topping,** thawed

Bring apricot nectar to a boil. Dissolve gelatin in nectar. Stir in cold water and pineapple with juice. Chill in a 9 x 13-inch pan until partially set, about 40 minutes. Stir in whipped topping. Chill until firm. Makes 12 servings.

CHERRY YOGURT SALAD

1 small box	**cherry gelatin**
1 container (6 ounces)	**cherry yogurt**
1 container (12 ounces)	**frozen whipped topping,** thawed
4	**bananas,** sliced*
3/4 cup	**chopped maraschino cherries**
1/2 cup	**chopped walnuts**
3 cups	**miniature marshmallows**

In a bowl, stir dry gelatin mix into yogurt. Stir in whipped topping and mix thoroughly but gently. Fold in the bananas, cherries, walnuts, and marshmallows. Chill for at least 15 minutes before serving. Makes 10–12 servings.

*To help prevent bananas from browning, sprinkle slices with a touch of lemon juice before stirring into salad.

CAKES

PINEAPPLE NUT CAKE

1 **yellow cake mix**
1 teaspoon **almond extract**

Topping:
1 can (20 ounces) **crushed pineapple**
1 small box **lemon gelatin**
1 container (12 ounces) **frozen whipped topping,** thawed
1/2 cup **chopped walnuts**

Make cake mix according to package directions, adding almond extract. Bake in two round cake pans.

Heat pineapple with juice in a saucepan. Add gelatin and stir until dissolved. Remove from heat and set aside to cool. When cooled, combine with whipped topping. Cover and refrigerate.

When cakes are cool, place one layer on a serving plate and spread with approximately 1 cup of the topping. Place second layer on top and then frost entire cake with remaining topping. Garnish with chopped nuts. Makes 10 servings.

POPPY SEED CAKE

1	**yellow cake mix**
1 small box	**vanilla instant pudding**
4	**eggs**
$1/2$ cup	**oil**
$1 1/2$ cups	**hot water**
2 tablespoons	**poppy seeds**

Icing:

$1/2$ cup	**lemon juice**
2 tablespoons	**lemon gelatin**
2 cups	**powdered sugar**

Preheat oven to 350 degrees F.

Beat cake mix, pudding mix, eggs, oil, and water in a large bowl on low speed for 30 seconds and then on medium speed for 2 minutes, scraping the sides of bowl occasionally. Stir in poppy seeds. Pour batter into a greased and floured Bundt pan and bake for 45–50 minutes, or until a toothpick inserted near the center comes out clean. Cool and then invert onto a serving plate.

In a small saucepan heat the lemon juice. Add gelatin and powdered sugar, a cup at a time, until all is incorporated and smooth. Drizzle icing over cooled cake. Makes 10–12 servings.

RASPBERRY CHOCOLATE CAKE

I	**devil's food cake mix**
I small box	**raspberry gelatin**
I cup	**boiling water**
$^1/_2$ cup	**cold water**
2 cups	**fresh raspberries** (optional)
I container (8 ounces)	**frozen whipped topping,** thawed

Prepare and bake cake as directed for a 9 x 13-inch pan. Allow to cool. Poke holes in cake with fork. Dissolve gelatin in I cup boiling water and then mix in 1/2 cup cold water. Pour gelatin mixture over cake. Chill 4 hours. Fold raspberries into whipped topping if using. Frost cake with whipped topping. Makes 12 servings.

SWEETHEART CAKE

1	**white cake mix**
1 teaspoon	**vanilla or almond extract**
2 tablespoons	**raspberry gelatin**
1/2 cup	**boiling water**
1 container (12 ounces)	**frozen whipped topping,** thawed
1 pint	**fresh raspberries**

Make cake according to package directions, adding either vanilla or almond extract. Bake in two round cake pans. When cakes are cool, dissolve gelatin in boiling water. Refrigerate until partially set and then combine gelatin and whipped topping. Place one layer of cake on a serving plate. Spread half the topping on top. Top with second layer of cake and spread remaining mixture over top. Leave sides of cake exposed to show the cake and whipped topping layers. Decorate top of layered cake with fresh raspberries. Makes 10–12 servings.

PEACH POKE CAKE

1	**white cake mix**
1 small box	**peach gelatin**
1 cup	**boiling water**
$^1/_2$ cup	**cold water**
1 container (8 ounces)	**frozen whipped topping,** thawed
2 cups	**sliced fresh or canned peaches**

Prepare and bake cake as directed for a 9 x 13-inch pan. Allow to cool.
Poke holes in cake with a fork. Dissolve gelatin in boiling water and
then mix in cold water. Pour gelatin mixture over cake. Chill 4 hours.
Top with whipped topping and garnish with peaches. Makes 12 servings.

STRAWBERRY-KIWI CAKE

I	**white cake mix**
I small box	**strawberry-kiwi gelatin**
I cup	**boiling water**
$^1/_2$ cup	**cold water**
I container (8 ounces)	**frozen whipped topping,** thawed
2 cups	**sliced strawberries** (optional)
2 to 3	**kiwifruit,** peeled and sliced (optional)

Prepare and bake cake as directed for a 9 x 13-inch pan. Allow to cool. Poke holes in cake with a fork. Dissolve gelatin in boiling water, then mix in cold water. Pour gelatin mixture over cake. Chill 4 hours. Top with whipped topping and garnish with fresh fruit if desired. Makes 12 servings.

PARTY LIME CUPCAKES

1	**Funfetti cake mix**
2 tablespoons	**lime gelatin**
1/2 cup	**boiling water**
1 small box	**vanilla instant pudding**
	candy sprinkles

Make cupcakes according to package directions. Dissolve gelatin in boiling water and cool until partially set. Make vanilla pudding. Stir gelatin into pudding and refrigerate for 1–2 hours, or until completely cool and thick enough to spread on cupcakes. Frost cupcakes with lime pudding and decorate with candy sprinkles. Makes 24 cupcakes.

BLACK FOREST CAKE

I	**devil's food cake mix**
I small box	**black cherry gelatin**
I cup	**boiling water**
1/2 cup	**cold water**
I container (8 ounces)	**frozen whipped topping,** thawed

Prepare and bake cake as directed for a 9 x 13-inch pan. Allow to cool. Poke holes in cake with a fork. Dissolve gelatin in boiling water, then mix in cold water. Pour gelatin mixture over cake. Chill 4 hours. Top with whipped topping. Makes 12 servings.

CARROT CAKE

I	**spice cake mix**
2 cups	**shredded carrots**
I can (8 ounces)	**crushed pineapple**
I small box	**orange jello**
I cup	**boiling water**
I cup	**cold water**
I container (12 ounces)	**cream cheese frosting**

Preheat oven to 350 degrees F.

Make cake mix according to package directions. When batter is prepared, stir in carrots and pineapple with juice. Bake in a 9 x 13-inch pan
for 30 minutes or until toothpick inserted in center comes out clean.
Allow to cool. Poke holes in cake with a fork. Dissolve gelatin in boiling
water; then stir in cold water. Pour gelatin mixture over cake. Chill 4
hours. Frost with cream cheese frosting. Makes 12 servings.

STRAWBERRY MARSHMALLOW CAKE

1	**white cake mix**
1 small box	**strawberry gelatin**
1 container (8 ounces)	**frozen whipped topping,** thawed
1 can (8 ounces)	**crushed pineapple**
3 cups	**miniature marshmallows**

Prepare and bake cake as directed for a 9 x 13-inch pan. Allow to cool.

In a large bowl, mix together dry gelatin mix and whipped topping. Stir in crushed pineapple with juice and marshmallows. Frost cake with topping. Makes 12 servings.

PINEAPPLE UPSIDE-DOWN CAKE

¹/₂ cup **butter**
I cup **brown sugar**
2 tablespoons **orange or lemon gelatin**
I can (15 ounces) **sliced pineapple,** drained
maraschino cherries
I **yellow cake mix**

Preheat oven to 375 degrees F.

Melt butter in the bottom of a 9 x 13-inch cake pan. Sprinkle brown sugar evenly over bottom. Sprinkle with dry gelatin mix. Arrange sliced pineapple to cover bottom. Fill each pineapple center with a maraschino cherry. Prepare cake mix according to package directions and pour over all. Bake for about 30 minutes, or when toothpick inserted in center comes out clean. Invert onto a serving platter. Makes 12 servings.

VERY LEMON CAKE

1	**lemon cake mix**
4	**eggs**
3/4 cup	**oil**
3/4 cup	**water**

Icing:

1/2 cup	**lemon juice**
2 tablespoons	**lemon gelatin**
2 cups	**powdered sugar**

Preheat oven to 350 degrees F.

Combine cake mix, eggs, oil, and water. Blend on low speed for 30 seconds and then on high speed for 2 minutes. Pour into a greased and floured 9 x 13-inch pan and bake for 30 minutes or until a toothpick inserted in the center comes out clean. Allow to cool.

Combine ingredients for icing in a small saucepan and bring to a boil. Boil 5 minutes and then drizzle over cake. Sprinkle more powdered sugar over top of completely cooled cake to garnish. Makes 12 servings.

ORANGE BLOSSOM CAKE

I	**yellow cake mix**
I box	**vanilla instant pudding**
I teaspoon	**vanilla extract**
I teaspoon	**almond extract**
I can (II ounces)	**mandarin oranges,** drained and smashed
I can (8 ounces)	**crushed pineapple**

Topping:

$^1/_2$ cup	**orange juice**
2 tablespoons	**orange gelatin**
$^1/_2$ pint	**whipping cream,** whipped and sweetened

Preheat oven to 350 degrees F.

Prepare batter according to package directions, adding pudding mix and extracts. When batter is completely blended, turn off mixer and fold in mandarin oranges and pineapple with juice by hand. Pour batter into a greased and floured Bundt pan and bake 50 minutes, or until a toothpick inserted in the center comes out clean.

To make the topping, bring orange juice to a boil and dissolve gelatin in juice. Chill until partially set. Fold gelatin into whipped cream and refrigerate. Before serving, top each slice of cake with a dollop of orange whipped cream. Makes 10–12 servings.

SWEET BERRY CAKE

1	**white cake mix**
1 cup	**vegetable oil**
$^1/_2$ cup	**milk**
3	**eggs**
1 package (12 ounces)	**frozen mixed berries,** thawed and drained

Icing:

$^1/_2$ cup	**butter**
1 pound	**powdered sugar**
5 tablespoons	**milk**
2 tablespoons	**any berry gelatin**

Preheat oven to 350 degrees F.

In a large mixing bowl, combine cake mix, oil, milk, and eggs. Mix well until blended. Fold in berries. Pour batter into two round or square cake pans. Bake for 25–30 minutes. Cool.

To make icing, combine butter, powdered sugar, milk, and gelatin in a small saucepan over medium heat until butter is melted. Drizzle over cake. Makes 12 servings.

PIES

FLUFFY STRAWBERRY PIE

1 small box	**strawberry gelatin**
3/4 cup	**boiling water**
1/2 cup	**ice cubes**
1 small box	**vanilla instant pudding**
3/4 cup	**cold milk**
3 cups	**frozen whipped topping,** thawed, divided
1 pint	**strawberries,** hulled and sliced
1	**baked 9-inch pie crust**

Completely dissolve gelatin in boiling water. Add ice cubes and stir until melted; set aside.

Prepare pudding mix as directed but using only 3/4 cup milk. Blend in gelatin using a wire whisk. Chill, if necessary, until thickened. Fold in 1 1/2 cups whipped topping and strawberries. Pour into crust. Freeze 1 hour or chill 3 hours in the refrigerator before serving. Garnish with remaining whipped topping and additional strawberries, if desired. Makes 8 servings.

ORANGE-LEMON PIE

2 small boxes **lemon gelatin**
I cup **boiling water**
2 **oranges,** juiced
I **lemon,** juiced
²/₃ cup **sugar**
I container (8 ounces) **frozen whipped topping,** thawed
I **premade graham cracker pie crust**

Dissolve gelatin in boiling water. Add juices and sugar. Refrigerate until very thick, about 45 minutes. Gently fold in whipped topping and then pour into crust. Chill until set. Makes 8 servings.

STRAWBERRY YOGURT PIE

1 small box	**strawberry gelatin**
2 containers (6 ounces each)	**strawberry yogurt**
1 container (8 ounces)	**frozen whipped topping,** thawed
1	**premade Oreo cookie pie crust**
1 cup	**sliced fresh strawberries**

In a bowl, combine dry gelatin mix with yogurt. Fold in whipped topping and then spread into crust. Place pie in the freezer until just before serving. Garnish with sliced strawberries. Makes 8 servings.

FROZEN LEMONADE PIE

1 small box **lemon gelatin**
1 package (8 ounces) **cream cheese,** softened
$^1/_2$ cup **frozen lemonade concentrate,** thawed
1 cup **frozen whipped topping,** thawed
1 **premade graham cracker pie crust**

In a bowl, beat the dry gelatin mix, cream cheese, and lemonade concentrate together until smooth. Fold in whipped topping and then pour into graham cracker crust and freeze. Makes 8 servings.

KEY LIME PIE

1 package (8 ounces) **cream cheese,** softened
1 can (14 ounces) **sweetened condensed milk**
1/2 small box **lime gelatin**
1 **lime,** zested and juiced
1 tablespoon **lemon juice**
1 **premade graham cracker pie crust**

Combine the cream cheese, condensed milk, dry gelatin mix, lime zest, and lime and lemon juices with a hand mixer until smooth and creamy. Pour into graham cracker crust and chill until set. Makes 8 servings.

PINEAPPLE CREAM CHEESE PIE

1 can (20 ounces) **crushed pineapple**
1 small box **lemon gelatin**
1 package (8 ounces) **cream cheese,** softened
1 **premade graham cracker pie crust,** chilled

Drain pineapple, reserving juice, and then add water to the reserved juice, if needed, to make 1 cup of liquid. Bring to a boil and add gelatin. Stir until dissolved.

With a hand mixer, blend cream cheese with half of the liquid gelatin. When smooth, pour into the chilled crust, arrange desired amount of crushed pineapple on top, and then pour remaining gelatin over top. Chill until set, about 3–4 hours. Makes 8 servings.

CHERRY-LEMON CREAM CHEESE PIE

1 package (8 ounces) **cream cheese,** softened
1 can (14 ounces) **sweetened condensed milk**
1/2 small box **cherry gelatin**
1 **small lemon,** zested and juiced
1 **premade graham cracker pie crust**
1 can **cherry pie filling**

Combine the cream cheese, condensed milk, dry gelatin mix, and lemon zest and juice with a hand mixer until smooth and creamy. Pour into graham cracker crust and chill until set. Spread pie filling over top and serve. Makes 8 servings.

MANDARIN ORANGE PIE

1 small box **orange gelatin**
2 containers (6 ounces each) **orange yogurt**
1 container (8 ounces) **frozen whipped topping,** thawed
1 **premade graham cracker pie crust**
1 can (11 ounces) **mandarin oranges,** drained

In a bowl, combine dry gelatin mix and yogurt. Fold in whipped topping. Spread into crust. Freeze pie 2–3 hours and remove from freezer just before serving. Garnish with mandarin oranges. Makes 8 servings.

PRETTY SPRING PIE

1 small box	**vanilla instant pudding mix**
1 small box	**gelatin,** any flavor
2 1/2 cups	**water**
1 container (8 ounces)	**frozen whipped topping,** thawed
1	**premade graham cracker pie crust**

In a saucepan, combine pudding mix, gelatin, and water over medium heat and bring to a boil. When mixture is thick and clear, remove from heat. Chill until slightly thickened and then fold in whipped topping. Pour mixture into pie crust, chill until firm, and then serve. Makes 8 servings.

FAVORITE PEACH PIE

I small box	**peach gelatin**
2 to 3 tablespoons	**sugar**
I cup	**boiling water**
I cup cold	**water**
1 1/2 cups	**sliced fresh or frozen peaches,** thawed
I	**baked 9-inch pie crust**
I container (8 ounces)	**frozen whipped topping,** thawed

Dissolve gelatin and sugar in boiling water and then add cold water. Chill until very thick. Fold in fruit and pour into pie crust. Chill until firm. Garnish with whipped topping. Makes 8 servings.

RASPBERRY DANISH PIE

1 cup	**sugar**
3 tablespoons plus 2 teaspoons	**cornstarch**
3 tablespoons	**light corn syrup**
4 tablespoons	**raspberry gelatin**
1 1/2 cups	**water**
2 to 3 cups	**fresh raspberries**
1	**baked 9-inch pie crust**

Stir together all ingredients except fruit and crust in a saucepan and then bring to a boil. Cool slightly and then stir in raspberries. Spoon Danish-coated raspberries into the baked pie crust with a slotted spoon, and then drizzle remaining Danish sauce over top just to fill pie. Chill until set and then serve. Makes 8 servings.

VARIATION: Replace raspberry gelatin and fresh raspberries with strawberry gelatin and fresh strawberries.

FROZEN CHERRY PIE

1 small box	**cherry gelatin**
1¼ cups	**boiling water**
1 pint	**vanilla ice cream**
1	**premade graham cracker pie crust**
1 can	**cherry pie filling**

Dissolve gelatin in boiling water. Add vanilla ice cream by the spoonful and stir each addition until melted. Chill until thickened but not set, about 45 minutes. Pour into pie crust and freeze. Remove from freezer and top individual slices with cherry pie filling before serving. Makes 8 servings.

CREAMY CRANBERRY PIE

1 cup	**cranberry juice**
1 small box	**cranberry or raspberry gelatin**
1 can (16 ounces)	**jellied cranberry sauce**
1 cup	**whipping cream,** whipped and sweetened
1	**premade graham cracker pie crust**

In a saucepan, bring juice to a boil. Remove from heat and add gelatin; stir until dissolved. In a separate bowl, beat the cranberry sauce for 1 minute, or until smooth. Add gelatin mixture and stir to combine. Chill until thickened but not set, about 45 minutes to 1 hour. Stir in whipped cream and then pour into crust. Chill until firm. Makes 8 servings.

FROZEN BLACK-BOTTOM RASPBERRY PIE

I small box	**raspberry gelatin**
I container (6 ounces)	**raspberry yogurt**
I package (8 ounces)	**cream cheese,** softened
I ¹/₂ cups	**frozen whipped topping,** thawed
	hot fudge
I	**premade Oreo cookie pie crust**

In a bowl, beat together the dry gelatin mix, yogurt, and cream cheese until smooth. Fold in whipped topping. Spread a thick layer of hot fudge over the bottom of pie crust. Pour pie filling over top and freeze. Garnish individual slices with more hot fudge if desired. Makes 8 servings.

SPOON DESSERTS

EASY CHEESECAKE

1 small box	**lemon gelatin**
1 cup	**boiling water**
1 package (8 ounces)	**cream cheese,** softened
1 cup	**sugar**
1 can (14 ounces)	**evaporated milk**
1	**premade graham cracker pie crust**

Stir gelatin in boiling water until dissolved. Cool in refrigerator until partially set. In a large bowl, cream together cream cheese, sugar, and evaporated milk until creamy. Pour gelatin mixture into cream cheese mixture and beat with a hand mixer on low speed until blended. Pour into crust. Chill 3–4 hours. Makes 10 servings.

STRAWBERRY CHEESECAKE SQUARES

Crust:

I cup	**graham cracker crumbs**
$^1/_4$ cup	**powdered sugar**
5 tablespoons	**butter,** melted

Filling:

I small box	**strawberry gelatin**
I cup	**boiling water**
I package (8 ounces)	**cream cheese,** softened
$^1/_2$ cup	**sugar**
I teaspoon	**vanilla**
I cup	**whipping cream,** whipped and sweetened

To make crust, combine graham cracker crumbs, powdered sugar, and butter and mix well. Save $^1/_4$ cup of mixture for topping. Press remaining amount into the bottom of a 7 x 9-inch pan.

To make filling, dissolve gelatin in boiling water. Chill until quite thickened, about I hour. Beat cream cheese, sugar, and vanilla with hand mixer until fluffy. Beat in thickened gelatin. Fold in whipped cream. Pour in pan and top with reserved topping. Chill for several hours and then cut into squares just before serving. Makes 9 servings.

VARIATION: Replace strawberry gelatin with lemon gelatin.

KEY LIME DESSERT

Crust:

2 cups	**Oreo cookie crumbs**
1/2 cup	**sugar**
1/2 cup	**butter,** melted

Filling:

1 large box	**lime gelatin**
2 cups	**boiling water**
2 packages (8 ounces each)	**cream cheese,** softened
1 cup	**sugar**
4 cups	**frozen whipped topping,** thawed, divided

Combine cookie crumbs, sugar, and butter and mix well. Press into the bottom of a 9 x 13-inch pan and set aside.

To make filling, dissolve gelatin in boiling water. Chill until quite thickened, about 1 hour. In a separate bowl, beat cream cheese and sugar on low with a hand mixer until fluffy. Beat in thickened gelatin. Fold in 2 cups whipped topping. Pour over crust and chill for several hours. Top with remaining whipped topping. Makes 12 servings.

RASPBERRY CREAM DESSERT

Crust:

2 1/2 cups	**graham cracker crumbs**
6 tablespoons	**sugar**
10 tablespoons	**butter,** melted

Filling:

1 package (8 ounces)	**cream cheese,** softened
1 cup	**powdered sugar**
2 containers (8 ounces each)	**frozen whipped topping,** thawed, divided
1 small box	**raspberry gelatin**
1/2 cup	**boiling water**
1 cup (8 ounces)	**raspberry yogurt**

In a bowl, combine the graham cracker crumbs, sugar, and butter for the crust. Reserve 3 tablespoons. Press remaining mixture into a 9 x 13-inch pan. Refrigerate for 15 minutes.

In a large mixing bowl, beat cream cheese and powdered sugar with a hand mixer until smooth. Whisk in 1 cup whipped topping. Spread this mixture over the prepared crust.

In another bowl dissolve gelatin in boiling water. Whisk in yogurt and remaining whipped topping from open container. When well blended, pour over cream cheese layer. Refrigerate for 1 hour. Spread second container whipped topping over raspberry layer; cover and refrigerate overnight. Sprinkle reserved topping over dessert. Makes 12 servings.

LEMON SHERBET SQUARES

Crust:

1 1/2 cups	**finely crushed vanilla wafers**
1/3 cup	**chopped pecans**
6 tablespoons	**butter or margarine,** melted

Filling:

1 large box	**lemon gelatin**
1 1/4 cups	**boiling water**
1 small box	**lemon instant pudding**
1 pint	**lemon sherbet or vanilla ice cream,** softened
2 cups	**frozen whipped topping,** thawed

To make crust, combine vanilla wafer crumbs, pecans, and butter or margarine. Reserve 1/4 cup crumb mixture; press remainder into a 10 x 6 x 1 1/2-inch baking dish. Chill.

Dissolve gelatin in boiling water; cool to lukewarm. Add dry pudding mix to gelatin; mix well. Add sherbet; beat with a hand mixer on low speed until thickened and nearly set. Fold in whipped topping. Turn into baking dish; sprinkle reserved crumb mixture on top. Chill at least 1 hour and then cut into squares. Makes 8–10 servings.

LEMON SOUFFLÉ

2 tablespoons	**graham cracker crumbs,** divided
I small box	**lemon gelatin**
$^3/_4$ cup	**boiling water**
I cup	**cottage cheese**
I package (8 ounces)	**light cream cheese**
2 cups	**frozen whipped topping,** thawed

Spray an 8- or 9-inch springform pan or a 9-inch pie plate with nonstick cooking spray. Sprinkle I tablespoon graham cracker crumbs on the bottom of the pan; set aside.

Place the gelatin in a medium bowl. Stir in the boiling water until the gelatin is completely dissolved, about 2 minutes. Pour the mixture into a blender or food processor fitted with a metal blade. Add cottage cheese and cream cheese. Blend or process on medium speed until smooth.

Pour the mixture into a large bowl and fold in the whipped topping to completely incorporate. Pour into prepared pan and smooth top. Sprinkle the remaining graham cracker crumbs over top. Refrigerate 4 hours or until set. Remove side of springform pan just before serving. Makes 8 servings.

STRAWBERRY TRIFLE

$^1/_2$	**angel food cake**
I small box	**vanilla instant pudding**
I small box	**strawberry gelatin**
I container (8 ounces)	**frozen whipped topping,** thawed
I pint	**fresh strawberries,** hulled and halved

Cut angel food cake into 1-inch cubes. Make pudding according to package directions. Make gelatin according to package directions and refrigerate until almost set.

In a trifle bowl or large glass serving bowl, layer the cake cubes and top with the pudding. Carefully spoon on the gelatin. Refrigerate for 30 minutes to 1 hour, or until gelatin is set. Before serving, top with whipped topping and strawberries. Makes 12–15 servings.

CHERRY COBBLER

2 cans (16 ounces each) **tart cherries,** drained
1 small box **cherry gelatin**
1 **yellow cake mix**
$^1/_4$ to $^1/_2$ cup **butter**
$^1/_2$ cup **water**

Preheat oven to 350 degrees F.

Pour fruit in the bottom of a 9 x 13-inch pan. Sprinkle dry gelatin mix over top and stir to mix with fruit. Sprinkle dry cake mix over fruit. Cut up butter and distribute over cake mix. Pour water over top. Bake for 45 minutes, or until the top is browned. Serve warm with whipped cream if desired. Makes 12 servings.

PEACH CRISP

1 package (16 ounces)	**frozen unsweetened peach slices**
2 tablespoons	**peach or lemon gelatin**
1/2 cup	**rolled oats**
1/2 cup	**brown sugar**
1/2 cup	**flour**
1/4 teaspoon	**cinnamon**
1/4 cup	**butter**

Preheat oven to 375 degrees F.

Thaw fruit but do not drain. Place in the bottom of a 7 x 9-inch baking dish. Sprinkle dry gelatin mix over top. In a medium bowl, combine oats, brown sugar, flour, and cinnamon. Cut in butter until mixture resembles coarse crumbs. Sprinkle over fruit in pan. Bake for 40–50 minutes, or until fruit is tender and bubbly and topping is brown. Serve with vanilla ice cream or fresh whipped cream if desired. Makes 4–6 servings.

CREAMY PUDDING

1 large box **gelatin,** any flavor
1 large box **Cook & Serve vanilla pudding**
1 container (8 ounces) **frozen whipped topping,** thawed

Make gelatin according to package directions and chill until partially set. In the meantime, make pudding according to package directions and cool. Fold partially set gelatin into pudding until smooth. Fold in whipped topping. Makes 8–10 servings.

PEACHY FROZEN YOGURT

I small box **peach gelatin**
I cup **boiling water**
3 cups **vanilla yogurt**

Dissolve gelatin in boiling water, stirring until completely dissolved, at least two minutes. Cool to room temperature. Combine with vanilla yogurt and freeze in an ice cream maker according to manufacturer's instructions. Makes 4 servings.

RASPBERRY ICE CREAM

1 small box	**raspberry gelatin**
1/2 cup	**boiling water**
1 package (10 ounces)	**frozen raspberries,** thawed and drained
1 cup	**whipping cream**
1 small box	**vanilla instant pudding**
2/3 cup	**sugar**
2 teaspoons	**vanilla**
1 quart	**whole milk**

Dissolve gelatin in boiling water. Stir in raspberries. In a separate bowl, mix together whipping cream, dry pudding mix, sugar, and vanilla. Stir into raspberry gelatin mixture. Pour into 1-gallon ice cream freezer container. Add milk and stir until blended. Freeze in an ice cream maker according to manufacturer's directions. Makes 8 servings.

STRAWBERRY-BANANA ICE CREAM

I small box	**strawberry gelatin**
I cup	**boiling water**
2 to 3	**bananas**
2 tablespoons	**lemon juice**
I package (16 ounces)	**frozen sliced strawberries,** thawed and drained
I cup	**sugar**
I cup	**sweetened condensed milk**
2 cups	**whipping cream**
2 cups	**whole milk**

In a large bowl, dissolve gelatin in boiling water. In a separate bowl, dice bananas and add lemon juice. In a third bowl, mix berries with sugar. Add bananas and berries to gelatin. Add remaining ingredients and freeze in an ice cream maker according to manufacturer's directions. Makes 8–10 servings.

VARIATION: Substitute I package (16 ounces) mixed berries for the strawberries.

LIME SORBET

I small box **lime gelatin**
I cup **boiling water**
3 cups **whole milk**
$^1/_2$ cup **sweetened condensed milk**
I **lime,** zested and juiced

Dissolve gelatin in boiling water; cool 20 minutes in refrigerator. In a large mixing bowl, add milk, sweetened condensed milk, lime zest and juice, and cooled gelatin. Mix thoroughly. Pour into ice cream maker and freeze according to manufacturer's instructions. Makes 6–8 servings.

RED HOT DESSERT

1 large box	**cherry gelatin**
1/2 cup	**cinnamon candies**
3 cups	**boiling water**
1 cup	**cold water**

Dissolve gelatin and cinnamon candies in boiling water until candies are completely dissolved. Stir in cold water. Pour into an 8 x 8-inch pan and chill until set. Makes 9 servings.

CARAMEL APPLE SQUARES

I large box **green apple gelatin**
I to 2 **bananas**, sliced
$^1/_2$ container (8 ounces) **frozen whipped topping,** thawed
caramel topping

Make gelatin according to package directions and chill in an 8 x 8-inch pan until set. Place sliced bananas evenly over top. Spread whipped topping over top and drizzle with caramel topping before serving. Makes 9 servings.

RAINBOW DESSERT

2 small boxes **cherry gelatin**
2 small boxes **orange gelatin**
2 small boxes **lemon gelatin**
2 small boxes **lime gelatin**
2 small boxes **grape gelatin**
2$^1/_2$ cups **frozen whipped topping,** thawed

Make first box cherry gelatin according to package directions. Pour into a large glass trifle bowl and chill until set. Make second box cherry gelatin according to package directions. Cool in refrigerator until completely cool. Whisk in $^1/_2$ cup whipped topping until smooth. Pour on top of set cherry gelatin in trifle bowl and chill until set. Repeat for orange, lemon, lime, and grape layers. Makes 12–14 servings.

NOTE: This dessert takes all day to make.

STRAWBERRY PRETZEL DESSERT

Crust:

1 1/2 cups	**crushed pretzels**
4 1/2 tablespoons	**sugar**
3/4 cup	**butter,** melted

Filling:

1 cup	**sugar**
2 packages (8 ounces each)	**cream cheese,** softened
1 container (8 ounces)	**frozen whipped topping,** thawed

Topping:

1 large box	**strawberry gelatin**
2 cups	**boiling water**
1 package (16 ounces)	**frozen strawberries**

Preheat oven to 350 degrees F.

Mix together pretzels, sugar, and melted butter. Press into the bottom of a 9 x 13-inch pan and bake for 10 minutes, or until lightly toasted. Set aside to cool completely.

In a medium bowl, beat sugar and cream cheese until smooth. Fold in whipped topping. Spread evenly over cooled crust. Refrigerate 30 minutes.

In another bowl, stir gelatin into boiling water. Mix in frozen strawberries and stir until thawed. Pour over cream cheese mixture in pan. Refrigerate until completely chilled, at least 1 hour. Makes 12–15 servings.

VARIATION: Use raspberry gelatin and frozen raspberries in place of strawberry gelatin and frozen strawberries.

Just for Fun

EDIBLE FISH BOWL

1	**brand-new glass fishbowl**, cleaned
3 small boxes	**berry blue gelatin**
	gummy sharks

Make gelatin according to package directions. Pour into fish bowl and chill until partially set. Push gummy sharks into the gelatin with the handle of a wooden spoon. Finish chilling until completely set. Makes 10 servings.

APPLE CHIPS

4 to 6 **apples**, cleaned
lemon juice
1 large box **gelatin,** any flavor

Using an apple peeler corer slicer, slice apples. Dip each apple slice into lemon juice and then dip one side of the apple in the dry gelatin mix. Spray the trays of a food dehydrator with nonstick cooking spray and set apple slices, gelatin side up, on the tray. Dehydrate for 4 hours and then check for crispness. If not desired crispness, check every 45 minutes until done.

VARIATION: Use 2 small boxes of different flavored gelatin.

CRISPY RICE SQUARES

1 large box	**gelatin,** any flavor
²/₃ cup	**light corn syrup**
4 tablespoons	**margarine**
8 to 10 cups	**Rice Krispies**

In a large pan, combine dry gelatin mix, corn syrup, and margarine. Bring mixture to a boil over medium heat, stirring constantly; remove from heat. Stir in Rice Krispies until well coated. Put in a buttered 9 x 13-inch pan and press down. Refrigerate 10–15 minutes and then cut into squares. Makes 12–15 servings.

GUMMY LOLLIPOPS

2 small boxes	**gelatin,** any flavor
1 ¼ cups	**boiling water**
4	**small paper cups** (5 ounces each)
6	**plastic straws,** cut in half

Dissolve gelatin in boiling water. Let stand for 15 minutes to cool. Pour into paper cups and refrigerate until firm. Carefully peel away paper cups from gelatin. With a knife dipped in warm water, cut each gelatin cup horizontally into 3 round slices. Insert straws into gelatin slices to make lollipops. Makes 12 lollipops.

FRUITY POPSICLES

1 small box	**grape gelatin**
1 envelope	**grape Kool-Aid drink mix**
1/2 cup	**sugar**
2 cups	**boiling water**
2 cups	**cold water**
12	**Popsicle sticks**

Dissolve gelatin, Kool-Aid, and sugar in boiling water. Add cold water and stir well. Pour into Popsicle molds or small paper cups. Freeze partially, insert sticks, and then freeze until firm, about 2–3 hours. Makes 12 Popsicles.

VARIATION: You can substitute any flavor gelatin and Kool-Aid that you like.

DOUBLE-ORANGE POPS

1 small box	**orange gelatin**
1/2 cup	**sugar**
2 cups	**boiling water**
2 cups	**cold orange juice**
12	**Popsicle sticks**

Dissolve gelatin and sugar in boiling water and then add juice. Pour into Popsicle molds or small paper cups. Freeze partially, insert sticks, and then freeze until firm, about 2–3 more hours. Makes 12 Popsicles.

POPCORN BALLS

I cup	**light corn syrup**
$^1/_2$ cup	**sugar**
I small box	**gelatin,** any flavor
$^1/_2$ cup	**coarsely chopped peanuts**
I cup	**Craisins or plain M&Ms** (optional)
9 to 10 cups	**plain popped popcorn**

Bring corn syrup and sugar to a boil. Remove from heat and add dry gelatin mix, stirring until dissolved. Add peanuts and Craisins or M&Ms if desired and pour over popcorn, mixing well to coat. Spray your hands with nonstick cooking spray and then quickly form 2- to 3-inch balls. Makes about 20–24 popcorn balls.

VARIATION: Omit the corn syrup and sugar. Melt $^1/_4$ cup butter and I bag (10 ounces) marshmallows in a saucepan. Stir in dry gelatin mix, nuts, and optional ingredients and then pour over popcorn and finish recipe as instructed above.

APRICOT SUGAR COOKIES

3/4 cup **butter-flavored shortening**
1 1/2 cups **sugar,** divided
2 **eggs**
1 teaspoon **vanilla**
1 small box **apricot gelatin**
2 1/2 cups **flour**
1 teaspoon **baking powder**
1 teaspoon **salt**

Preheat oven to 400 degrees F.

In large bowl, cream shortening and 3/4 cup sugar together with electric hand mixer. Add eggs, vanilla, and dry gelatin mix; mix well. Stir in flour, baking powder, and salt. Shape dough into 1-inch balls. Place on a greased baking sheet and slightly flatten. Sprinkle generously with remaining sugar. Bake for 8–10 minutes. Makes 24–30 cookies.

VARIATION: Combine remaining sugar with a few dashes of cinnamon and then sprinkle over cookies just before baking; when cooled, frost with cream cheese frosting.

LEMON POPPY SEED COOKIES

4 cups	**flour**
1 teaspoon	**baking powder**
1 1/2 cups	**butter or margarine**
1 cup	**sugar**
2 small boxes	**lemon gelatin**
1	**egg**
1 teaspoon	**almond extract**
2 tablespoons	**poppy seeds**

Preheat oven to 400 degrees F.

Sift flour with baking powder and set aside. In a large bowl, cream the butter and then gradually add sugar and 1 box gelatin, creaming well after each addition. Add egg and almond extract; beat well. Gradually add flour mixture, mixing after each addition until smooth. Gently stir in poppy seeds and then roll dough into 1-inch balls and place on ungreased baking sheets. Slightly flatten dough balls and then sprinkle with dry gelatin mix from the remaining box. Bake about 13–14 minutes, or until golden brown at edges. Store in a loosely covered container. Makes about 60 cookies.

COOKIE SWIRLS

3/4 cup **butter,** softened
1/2 cup **sugar**
1/2 cup **sour cream**
2 cups **flour**
1/2 teaspoon **baking soda**
I small box **grape or black cherry gelatin**

Preheat oven to 350 degrees F.

Cream butter and sugar together; add sour cream. In a separate bowl, mix together flour and baking soda. Add to the sour cream mixture. Blend well and chill 2 hours or overnight.

Divide dough in half and roll each half into a rectangle. Brush rectangles with water and sprinkle each with 1/2 package dry gelatin mix. Roll up. Chill for 1–2 hours.

Cut dough into slices. Place on greased cookie sheets and bake 10–12 minutes. Makes about 24 cookies.

STRAWBERRY PIZZA

1 tube	**sugar cookie dough**
1 package (8 ounces)	**cream cheese,** softened
3/4 cup	**powdered sugar**
1 container (8 ounces)	**frozen whipped topping,** thawed
1 small box	**strawberry gelatin**
1 cup	**boiling water,** divided
4 tablespoons	**cornstarch**
3 to 4 cups	**sliced strawberries**

Preheat oven to 400 degrees F.

Press sugar cookie dough onto a pizza pan. Bake for 12–15 minutes. Put cream cheese in a bowl and then add powdered sugar a little at a time, stirring until creamed together. Fold in whipped topping and then spread on cooled crust.

Mix gelatin in 1/2 cup boiling water until dissolved. In a saucepan over medium-high heat, dissolve cornstarch in the remaining 1/2 cup boiling water. Stir gelatin mixture into cornstarch mixture and cook until thick. Stir in strawberries and allow to cool. Pour over cream cheese mixture and refrigerate until cool. Makes 12 servings.

MORMON SALAD

I large box	**lime gelatin**
2 cups	**shredded carrots**
I can (20 ounces)	**crushed pineapple**

Prepare gelatin according to package directions. Stir in carrots and pineapple with juice; chill in a 9 x 13-inch pan until set. Makes 12–15 servings.

FINGER JELL-O

3 small boxes **gelatin,** any flavor
4 small packages **Knox unflavored gelatin**
4 cups **boiling water**

Dissolve gelatin in boiling water. Pour into a 9 x 13-inch pan and refrigerate until firm. Cut into squares or into shapes with cookie cutters and eat with fingers. Makes about 24 servings.

DRINKS

BANANA WHIP

1 small box	**lemon gelatin**
¹/₂ cup	**milk**
1	**banana,** peeled
1 container (6 ounces)	**banana or vanilla yogurt**
1 ¹/₂ cups	**ice**

Mix all ingredients together in a blender until smooth and frothy. Pour into glasses and serve immediately. Makes 2–4 servings.

PURPLE COW

$^{1}/_{2}$ small box **grape gelatin**
1 cup **milk**
1 cup **grape juice**
2 cups **vanilla ice cream**
6 to 8 **ice cubes**

Combine all ingredients together in a blender until smooth. Serve immediately. Makes 4–6 servings.

ORANGE JULIUS

1 1/4 cups **orange juice**
3/4 cup **milk**
2 tablespoons **orange gelatin**
1/4 cup **sugar**
1 to 1 1/2 cups **ice**

In a blender, combine all ingredients in the order listed above and then blend until smooth. Serve immediately. Makes 4–6 servings.

CHERRY LEMONADE SLUSH

1 large box	**cherry gelatin**
2 cups	**boiling water**
2 cups	**sugar**
2 envelopes	**red Kool-Aid**
2 cups	**pineapple juice**
1 can (12 ounces)	**frozen lemonade concentrate,** thawed
2^1/$_2$ quarts	**water**
2 bottles (2 liters each)	**lemon-lime soda**

Dissolve gelatin in boiling water. Mix together with remaining ingredients except soda and freeze overnight. Remove from the freezer an hour or so before serving. Scoop slush into cups and pour cold soda over top. Makes 24–30 servings.

SWEET-AND-SOUR BERRY SLUSH

¹/₂ cup	**sugar**
1 small box	**strawberry gelatin**
2 cups	**boiling water**
2 cups	**sliced strawberries**
1 cup	**pineapple juice**
1 can (12 ounces)	**frozen lemonade concentrate,** thawed
1 can (12 ounces)	**frozen limeade concentrate,** thawed
2 cups	**water**
1 bottle (2 liters)	**ginger ale**

In a large bowl, dissolve sugar and gelatin in boiling water. In a blender, mix strawberries and pineapple juice until smooth and then stir into gelatin mixture. Stir in thawed concentrates and water, and then cover and freeze for 6–8 hours or overnight. About 1 hour before serving, remove from freezer. Scoop slush into cups and then pour cold ginger ale over top. Makes 16–20 servings.

ORANGE-PINEAPPLE COLADA

1 small box **island pineapple gelatin**
1 small can (6 ounces) **frozen orange juice concentrate**
1 cup **coconut milk**
1 cup **milk**
10 to 12 **ice cubes**

Combine all ingredients together in a blender until smooth. Serve immediately. Makes 4–6 servings.

CRAN-RASPBERRY PUNCH

4 cups **cold cranberry juice cocktail**
1 cup **cold orange juice**
1 small box **sugar-free raspberry gelatin**
1 liter **cold lemon-lime soda**

In a large pitcher, mix together juices and dry gelatin mix. Pour in the lemon-lime soda and stir. Serve immediately. Makes 10–12 servings.

ICY LEMON-LIME REFRESHER

1 to 2 cups	**ice**
2 cups	**cold lemon-lime soda**
1 small box	**lime gelatin**
2	**limes,** juiced and pulp reserved
1 tablespoon	**lemon juice**

Pour ice, soda, and dry gelatin mix into a blender. Add lime juice and pulp and lemon juice. Blend for 30–60 seconds or until slushy and smooth. Serve immediately. Makes 4–6 servings.

RASPBERRY SMOOTHIE

1 small box **raspberry gelatin**
1 to 1½ cups **milk**
2 cups **vanilla ice cream**

Combine all ingredients together in a blender until smooth and creamy.
Serve immediately. Makes 4–6 servings.

BUMBLE SHAKES

¹/₂ cup **boiling water**
1 small box **berry blue gelatin**
2 cups **vanilla ice cream**
¹/₂ to 1 cup **milk**
¹/₂ to 1 cup **crushed ice**

Pour boiling water in a blender and add dry gelatin mix. Cover and blend on medium speed for 1 minute; scrape the sides. With blender running, add ice cream by the spoonful. When done, gradually add the milk and ice until the desired consistency has been reached, blending after each addition. Serve immediately. Makes 4 servings.

NOTES

NOTES

Metric Conversion Chart

Liquid and Dry Measures

U.S.	Canadian	Australian
¼ teaspoon	1 mL	1 ml
½ teaspoon	2 mL	2 ml
1 teaspoon	5 mL	5 ml
1 tablespoon	15 mL	20 ml
¼ cup	50 mL	60 ml
⅓ cup	75 mL	80 ml
½ cup	125 mL	125 ml
⅔ cup	150 mL	170 ml
¾ cup	175 mL	190 ml
1 cup	250 mL	250 ml
1 quart	1 liter	1 litre

Temperature Conversion Chart

Fahrenheit	Celsius
250	120
275	140
300	150
325	160
350	180
375	190
400	200
425	220
450	230
475	240
500	260

ABOUT THE AUTHORS

Jennifer Adams is the author of five previous books, including *Wedding Showers* and *Baby Showers*. She loves good books, old movies, autumn leaves, expensive chocolate, and hosting parties for family and friends. Jennifer received her degree in English literature from the University of Washington. She works as a writer and editor, and lives with her husband, Virgil Grillone, in Salt Lake City. Her favorite gelatin is Blueberry Cream Cheese Salad.

Melissa Barlow is also the author of *101 Things To Do With a Salad* and *Easy Cut-Up Cakes for Kids*. She loves spending time with family and friends, reading, shopping, watching movies, and yummy food! Melissa received her bachelor's degree in journalism from Weber State University. She works as a writer and editor, and lives with her husband, Todd, in Bountiful, Utah. Her favorite gelatin is Strawberry Pretzel Dessert.